Editor
Gisela Lee, M.A.

Managing Editor
Karen J. Goldfluss, M.S. Ed.

Editor-in-Chief
Sharon Coan, M.S. Ed.

Illustrator
Kevin McCarthy

Cover Artist
Brenda DiAntonis

Art Manager
Kevin Barnes

Art Director
CJae Froshay

Imaging
Craig Gunnell

Product Manager
Phil Garcia

Publishers
Rachelle Cracchiolo, M.S. Ed.
Mary Dupuy Smith, M.S. Ed.

Spotlight on America: Elections

Author

Robert W. Smith

Teacher Created Materials, Inc.
6421 Industry Way
Westminster, CA 92683
www.teachercreated.com
ISBN-0-7439-3217-X

©2004 Teacher Created Materials, Inc.
Made in U.S.A.

Table of Contents

| 1750 | 1800 | 1850 | 1900 | 1950 | 2000 |

Introduction

The *Spotlight on America* series is designed to introduce some of the seminal events in American history to students in the fourth through eighth grades. Reading in the content area is enriched with a balanced variety of activities in written language, social studies, and oral expression. The series is designed to make history literally come alive in your classroom and take root in the minds of your students. The reading selections and comprehension questions serve to introduce presidential elections and American democracy. They set the stage for activities in other subject areas.

The presidency of the United States was an invention of the founding fathers who wrote the Constitution of the United States. They wanted to create a strong executive whose powers were limited by law and checked by other branches of government.

The Constitution allowed the states to decide how the presidential electors in the electoral college would be chosen. Some were chosen directly by state legislatures. Some were elected in general state-wide elections. These elections allowed only a select group of white men to vote. These men were usually educated and owned property. The voters did not include Native Americans, African-Americans, women, children, and people who didn't own property or have money. However, the system these men created has been expanded to give the right to vote to virtually all adult American citizens.

The United States is the oldest functioning democracy on earth and one of the oldest governments. The nation still operates under the separation of powers the founders devised. The legal protections against tyranny have worked well for over 200 years. This democratic government has endured war, severe economic depressions, civil war, and other great crises but the nation has survived and flourished.

The writing and oral language activities in this book are designed to help students learn how to function effectively in a democratic society. The activities encourage students to engage in critical thinking projects related to their nation and to express themselves cogently, fluently, and effectively in both oral and written venues.

The research activities are intended to bring students figuratively into the suits and boots of presidents as diverse as Thomas Jefferson and George W. Bush, Abraham Lincoln, and Harry Truman, Franklin Roosevelt, and Andrew Jackson. The culminating activities aim to acquaint students with the processes of democratic action and the rich history of the United States as it enters the 21st century.

Enjoy using this book with your students and look for other books in this series.

Teacher Lesson Plans

Reading Comprehension—Electing a President

Objective: Students will demonstrate fluency and comprehension in reading historically based text.

Materials

- copies of Electing a President (pages 7 and 8)
- copies of reading comprehension quiz entitled Electing a President (page 20)
- additional reading selections from books, encyclopedias, and Internet sources for enrichment

Procedure

1. Reproduce and distribute Electing a President (pages 7 and 8). Review pre-reading skills by briefly reviewing text and encouraging students to underline, make marginal notes and list questions, and highlight unfamiliar words as they read.

2. Assign the reading as classwork or homework. Allow adequate time for students to finish.

3. Talk about these discussion questions or others of your choosing with the students.
   - Why might an interested candidate decide not to run for President of the United States?
   - Why is it important for a candidate to have a good team to help during the campaign?
   - Would you want to run for president? Give your reasons.
   - What are the advantages and disadvantages of the electoral college?

Assessment—Have students complete the reading comprehension quiz entitled Electing a President (page 20). Correct and evaluate the quiz for student understanding.

Reading Comprehension—The History of Presidential Elections

Objective: Students will demonstrate fluency and comprehension in reading historically based text.

Materials

- copies of The History of Presidential Elections (pages 9–12)
- copies of reading comprehension quiz entitled The History of Presidential Elections (page 21)
- additional reading selections from books, encyclopedias, and Internet sources for enrichment

Procedure

1. Reproduce and distribute The History of Presidential Elections (pages 9–12). Review pre-reading skills by briefly reviewing text and encouraging students to underline, make marginal notes and list questions, and highlight unfamiliar words as they read.

2. Assign the reading as classwork or homework. Allow adequate time for students to finish.

3. Talk about these discussion questions or others of your choosing with the students.
   - Which president do you most admire? Why?
   - Which presidential election had the most unfair result? Explain your reasoning.
   - Should a candidate accept defeat in a close election even if he felt he won? Give your reasons.

Assessment—Have students complete the reading comprehension quiz entitled The History of Presidential Elections (page 21). Correct and evaluate the quiz for student understanding.

Teacher Lesson Plans *(cont.)*

Reading Comprehension—American Elections

Objective: Students will demonstrate fluency and comprehension in reading historically based text.

Materials

- copies of American Elections (pages 13–15)
- copies of reading comprehension quiz entitled American Elections (page 22)
- additional reading selections from books, encyclopedias, and Internet sources for enrichment

Procedure

1. Reproduce and distribute American Elections (pages 13–15). Review pre-reading skills by briefly reviewing text and encouraging students to underline, make marginal notes and list questions, and highlight unfamiliar words as they read.
2. Assign the reading as class work or homework. Allow adequate time for students to finish.
3. Talk about these discussion questions or others of your choosing with the students.
   - Why would a candidate choose to run as an Independent?
   - Why are terms of office specified for elective positions?
   - How long do you think a president should serve? Should it be longer or shorter than four years?

Assessment—Have students complete the reading comprehension quiz entitled American Elections (page 22). Correct and evaluate the quiz for student understanding.

Reading Comprehension—The Right to Vote

Objective: Students will demonstrate fluency and comprehension in reading historically based text.

Materials

- copies of The Right to Vote (pages 16 and 17)
- copies of reading comprehension quiz entitled The Right to Vote (page 23)
- additional reading selections from books, encyclopedias, and Internet sources for enrichment

Procedure

1. Reproduce and distribute The Right to Vote (pages 16 and 17). Review pre-reading skills by briefly reviewing text and encouraging students to underline, make marginal notes and list questions, and highlight unfamiliar words as they read.
2. Assign the reading as classwork or homework. Allow adequate time for students to finish.
3. Talk about these discussion questions or others of your choosing with the students.
   - Why should every eligible American vote?
   - Why do you think so many people choose not to vote?
   - Which amendment to the Constitution was most important in opening up the right to vote?

Assessment—Have students complete the reading comprehension quiz entitled The Right to Vote (page 23). Correct and evaluate the quiz for student understanding.

Teacher Lesson Plans *(cont.)*

Reading Comprehension—Democracy

Objective: Students will demonstrate fluency and comprehension in reading historically based text.

Materials

- copies of Democracy (pages 18 and 19)
- copies of reading comprehension quiz entitled Democracy (page 24)
- additional reading selections from books, encyclopedias, and Internet sources for enrichment

Procedure

1. Reproduce and distribute Democracy (pages 18 and 19). Review pre-reading skills by briefly reviewing text and encouraging students to underline, make marginal notes and list questions, and highlight unfamiliar words as they read.

2. Assign the reading as classwork or homework. Allow adequate time for students to finish.

3. Talk about these discussion questions or others of your choosing with the students.
   - What can you do to ensure that democracy works in this country?
   - What would life in a tyranny be like? Give some examples.
   - Why are the rights of a minority so important in preserving a democracy?

Assessment—Have students complete the reading comprehension quiz entitled Democracy (page 24). Correct and evaluate the quiz for student understanding.

Electing a President

Deciding to Run

An individual who wants to be elected President of the United States today needs strong public support. The candidate starts by assessing his or her chances for victory and the personal costs. Political opponents and their allies may tarnish the reputation of the candidate with unpleasant details of an individual's personal life. Spouses and children may also be hurt by comments and revelations. All presidential candidates build a team of advisors and aides who help them conduct a campaign. Members of the team advise them on issues, assist in fund-raising, suggest strategies for communicating their message, and keep the press informed.

Primaries and Caucuses

Today, a majority of states have primary elections. These elections are scheduled in the year of a presidential election—allow the members of a party in a state to select the candidate they wish. The earliest primary is traditionally in New Hampshire. The primary elections often indicate which candidate has popular support, especially within the candidate's party. A few states use the caucus system where individual party members meet to elect delegates who will pledge to vote for a candidate at the national convention. Traditionally, the first presidential caucus is held in Iowa.

The National Convention

The formal selection of a presidential candidate occurs at a national party convention. Thousands of party representatives selected in primaries, caucuses, and by state party members convene in a major city to formally elect their candidate. Often the convention just officially names the candidate who has already won a majority of the voting delegates to the convention by winning primaries, caucuses, and support from state party organizations.

Occasionally, as in the 1960 Democratic convention, the leading candidate has not secured the nomination. A good deal of political horse-trading often occurs in conventions of this type. Sometimes, one candidate will offer another candidate a position as a vice presidential nominee or a job in his future administration in exchange for the support of the other candidate's followers. In 1960 John Kennedy offered Lyndon Johnson the vice presidency in exchange for his support.

The Campaign

National conventions are usually held in late July or August. The official presidential campaign starts after Labor Day in early September. For two months the major candidates give speeches, run political ads on television, radio, and in the newspapers, and travel extensively to meet the people and convince the voters to support them. They also spend a great deal of time trying to raise money for their campaigns.

Electing a President *(cont.)*

Debates

Presidential debates were staged in some early elections. The debates between Lincoln and his opponent, Stephen Douglas, were especially famous. Debates became a feature of modern elections when John Kennedy and Richard Nixon engaged in a series of spirited and highly important televised debates. Most of the presidential elections since then have had debates. These debates often influence voters' perceptions of the abilities and personality of each candidate.

Election Day

Presidential elections are held on the first Tuesday after the first Monday in November every four years. Individual voting precincts in each state count the ballots and report the results to an election board which certifies the results. In elections where one candidate is the clear winner, the candidate often knows before he goes to bed that night if he has won. Close elections may involve several days or weeks of recounting.

Electoral College

Members of the electoral college meet in December to cast their ballots. They represent the winning candidate in their state. They agreed to support the candidate whose name was attached to their slate of electors. The actual determination of a president's election is made by these electors. In almost every state, if a candidate wins the most popular votes in the state, he receives all of the electoral votes in a state. For example, a victory by a few hundred votes in a large state such as California would mean the candidate won all of California's electoral college votes.

Inauguration

The newly elected president is inaugurated at 12 noon on January 20th in the year following a presidential election. He formally takes the oath of office and assumes the responsibilities of the presidency.

The History of Presidential Elections

1789 – George Washington

George Washington led his country through six years of war against Great Britain. He refused to assume power during the civil unrest that followed the war. Washington chaired the Constitutional Convention that defined the presidency and designed the methods of presidential election. Therefore, it was no surprise that the 69 electors who met in New York on February 4, 1789, voted unanimously to elect George Washington as President of the United States. Among both the people and the nation's leaders, Washington was universally admired for his service. President Washington had no major opposition in either of his elections. No other presidential election would be so tame.

1800 – Jefferson, Adams, and Burr

After Washington's retirement from office, presidential elections became hotly contested affairs. One of the most confusing elections occurred in 1800. Two political parties had developed. John Adams represented the Federalists who favored business, the wealthy, and a strong national government while Thomas Jefferson represented the Democratic Republicans who were more attuned to the interests of individual state governments, farmers, laboring men, and small businessmen.

The Democratic Republicans backing Jefferson clearly defeated Adams' Federalists, but a fluke in the law sent the election to the House of Representatives. The electors had cast an equal number of votes for both Jefferson and Aaron Burr who was expected to be named vice president. The tied vote had to be settled in the House of Representatives where many Federalist congressmen voted for Burr despite the fact that Republican electors had clearly intended Jefferson to be president.

Hamilton Sides with Jefferson

It took 36 votes in the House before the issue was finally settled, and Thomas Jefferson became president and Aaron Burr vice president. Alexander Hamilton, a political opponent of Jefferson, was nonetheless instrumental in defeating Burr, a man whose character he detested. (Burr would later kill Hamilton in a duel.) The 12th Amendment to the Constitution was passed before the next presidential election and required that electors use different and distinct ballots for president and vice president.

The History of Presidential Elections *(cont.)*

1824 – John Quincy Adams vs. Andrew Jackson

The next really contested presidential election occurred in 1824 between John Quincy Adams and Andrew Jackson. Adams represented eastern business and political interests and Jackson was the hero of the frontier. He championed the interests of pioneers, small farm owners, and laborers, many of whom had demanded and gradually acquired the right to vote in many states, especially in the newly formed frontier states of the West.

Jackson won 99 electoral votes and more popular votes than Adams who had 84 electoral votes. Another 78 electoral votes were split among two other candidates, Henry Clay and William Crawford. Because no one had a majority of electoral votes, the election was resolved in the House of Representatives with a victory for Adams.

Jackson and his supporters always felt he had been robbed and that Clay and Adams had made a deal. Four years later, Jackson would win the presidency in a clear victory over Adams. Part of his victory was due to the growth in the number of men eligible to vote. In the 1824 election, about 270,000 popular votes were cast all together. Four years later, Jackson alone would receive almost 650,000 votes and Adams about 510,000 popular votes.

National Party Conventions

The first national party conventions were held in 1832 when Jackson ran for his second term. These conventions became the formal occasion for selecting presidential candidates, although the candidate may have already secured all the necessary support. These conventions would become a tradition. Every four years political conventions assemble to formally announce their candidates for the presidency.

1860 – Abraham Lincoln—A Nation Divided

By 1860 the nation was being torn apart by the issue of slavery. Compromises for admitting slave states and free states had been attempted. Members of Congress had been involved in fist fights and had even been assaulted over the issue. The political battle between the North and South over the issue of slavery had led to the rise of the Republican Party, which was solidly anti-slavery.

The History of Presidential Elections (cont.)

A Bittersweet Victory

Abraham Lincoln represented the Republican party in a four-way battle for the presidency against Democrat Stephen A. Douglas and two other candidates. The campaign against Lincoln was particularly bitter and filled with nasty accusations and hatred. Lincoln won a clear majority of the electoral ballots and the highest popular vote with almost 1,900,000 votes out of a total of about 4,500,000 total votes, but the victory was bittersweet.

Between the election in early November 1860 and Lincoln's inauguration on March 4, 1861, seven southern states, led by South Carolina, seceded from the Union. The Confederate government led by President Jefferson Davis was created. The Civil War began in April and lasted four years, ending a few days after Lincoln's second inauguration in 1865 and just before his assassination.

1876 – Tilden Defeats Hayes

In the election of 1876, Samuel Tilden, the Democratic nominee for president, received a quarter of a million more popular votes than the Republican, Rutherford B. Hayes. More than eight million popular votes were cast. Election returns in three southern states were disputed with accusations of fraud on both sides. No one had a clear majority of electoral votes. The election was again thrown into Congress who established a special electoral commission. This group decided eight to seven to give the disputed votes to Hayes. Democrats felt that their candidate had been cheated of the presidency but reluctantly accepted the results.

1912 – Teddy Roosevelt Tries for a Third Term

The first state law providing a presidential primary was passed by Oregon in 1910. A primary election allows voters to vote for the candidate in their party whom they prefer to be the nominee for the presidency. By the election of 1912, 10 states had presidential primaries. Theodore Roosevelt, who had served two terms as president before he retired, decided to run for a third term against William Howard Taft, the incumbent Republican president. Roosevelt, who was always popular with the people, won 9 of the 10 primaries, but Taft had the support of the professional politicians who controlled most of the remaining states, and he became the nominee of his party at the national convention.

The History of Presidential Elections *(cont.)*

Bull Moose Beaten

Theodore Roosevelt decided to start his own political party which he called the Bull Moose party. Roosevelt drew more votes than Taft, but they divided the votes of Republican voters and Democrat Woodrow Wilson won the election. The total size of the popular vote had grown considerably since Lincoln's election to about 14,000,000 votes.

Modern Elections

Modern presidential elections have also often been the subject of disputes. Franklin Roosevelt sparked controversy by running for both a third and a fourth term of office. No president before him had won such an election. Roosevelt won all four terms.

Harry Truman shocked his political enemies in 1948. Most polls and professional politicians were certain that he would lose to the Republican candidate, Thomas E. Dewey. One newspaper, the *Chicago Tribune*, even headlined his defeat. Truman gleefully held up the newspaper headline the day after his election.

John F. Kennedy defeated Richard Nixon in 1960 by about 100,000 votes out of more than 68 million votes. Studies showed that a switch of a few thousand votes in some critical states would have swung the election to Nixon.

Richard Nixon's concerns about his reelection in 1972 led to a break-in at the Democratic National Committee headquartered at the Watergate Apartments in Washington, D.C. The resulting scandal implicated many high level members of his administration and led to Nixon's resignation from the presidency to avoid impeachment.

Bush vs. Gore

In one of the most closely contested elections in American history, George W. Bush defeated Al Gore for the presidency in the 2000 election. Gore actually received about one-half million more popular votes than Bush out of about 101 million votes cast for the two men. The winner needed 270 electoral votes. Bush won the disputed election in Florida after a series of legal challenges that ended up in the Supreme Court. His final electoral total was 271 votes.

American Elections

Governing a Nation

In the United States, citizens govern themselves by choosing the people who make and enforce the laws under which they live. The Founding Fathers who wrote the Constitution of the United States deliberately created a system where no person or group of people could take power and hold it against the will of the people. They established three branches of government—legislative, executive, and judicial—so that each branch would be held in check by the other two branches. In addition many functions of government are under state, not federal, control. Within a state, most of the everyday laws under which people live are controlled by local governments.

Who Gets Elected

Citizens select most of their leaders for all levels of government. They may be selected at the same election or at elections held solely for one level of government. There are approximately 85,000 state and local governments in the United States with approximately 500,000 elected officials. Below is a list of some of the positions for which citizens vote.

Federal Government
- President of the United States
- Vice President of the United States
- United States Senator (two per state)
- United States Representative in the House of Representatives

State Government
- Governor
- Lieutenant Governor
- State Attorney General (Legal Officer)
- State Comptroller (Financial Officer)
- State Senator
- State Assemblyman
- State Judges
- Individuals in charge of water districts, elections, and other duties

Local Government
- City Mayor
- City Council Members
- County Officers
- City and County Judges
- Sheriff or Police Chief
- School Board Members
- Members of local water districts, boards, and commissions

American Elections *(cont.)*

Terms of Office

Most elections are held at regularly scheduled times although special elections may be held to fill vacancies in local, state, or even national positions. Most positions have specified terms of office. A President of the United States serves four years. Presidential elections will be held in 2004, 2008, and every four years thereafter. Presidents and many other officials are elected at these general elections. United States senators serve six years in office. Only one-third of the 100 U. S. Senators are up for election in federal elections held every two years. Members of Congress serving in the House of Representatives are elected every two years. Governors usually serve four-year terms although a few states still have two-year terms. Virtually all other public officials have terms of office, usually ranging from one to four years.

Political Parties

Most federal and state offices are held by individuals who belong to one of the two main political parties, the Democrats and the Republicans. Members of a party who want to hold elective office usually participate in primary elections which are held several months before a general election. Usually, only members of a party can vote in their party's primary election. Then the representatives of each party will compete against each other in the general election.

American Elections *(cont.)*

Third Parties/Independents

Sometimes members of a third party will also compete for an office. Some individuals may form their own party or join a group unhappy with the two main national parties. Occasionally, a candidate of these third parties will win. Even if they don't win, they may affect the election. The third party candidacy of Ross Perot received 19% of the popular vote in the 1992 presidential election. His campaign may have helped Bill Clinton defeat George Bush in that election. Of the 50 states, often one or two are led by governors who ran as independent or third party candidates.

Nonpartisan Elections

Many local elections are not partisan which means that individuals do not have to declare a party affiliation and may not belong to either major party. People select leaders based on the reputation of the person running and their positions on local issues. Many city and county offices are nonpartisan races as are most school board elections. School boards determine the educational policy of the local school system. Other local boards and commissions, such as water districts and sanitation commissions, are also nonpartisan offices. So are many local and state judicial offices.

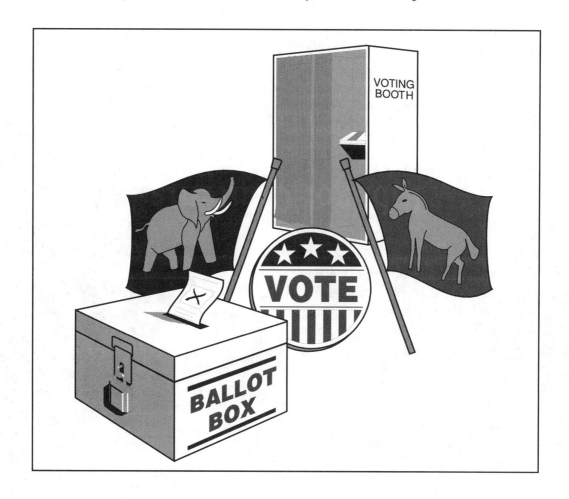

| 1750 | 1800 | 1850 | 1900 | 1950 | 2000 |

The Right to Vote

Early Restrictions

Most of the Founding Fathers believed that voting should be restricted to white men who owned property or who were wealthy and respected in their community. The first popular vote count with reliable figures is the 1824 election of John Quincy Adams. Votes for the four candidates together only totaled about 350,000 out of a population of about 10 million people. This is about 3% of the population. Among those who were not eligible to vote were women, African Americans, American Indians, children, those who lacked property, non-citizens, and criminals.

Suffrage Expands

In the early 1800s, additional American men gradually acquired the franchise, the right to vote. Laborers who didn't own property, poor farmers, and pioneers in the new western states convinced state authorities to extend voting rights to them. In 1860 about 4.5 million men voted in the presidential election out of a total population of about 31 million people. This was about 14% of the population.

The 15th Amendment

The 15th Amendment to the Constitution was passed during the Reconstruction period after the Civil War. This amendment was intended to ensure that newly freed slave men were granted the right to vote. Many African Americans in the South were able to exercise this right until the withdrawal of federal troops in the 1870s. Most of the former Confederate states then enacted laws or used force and coercion to prevent freedmen from voting. These methods included the use of a poll tax, literacy requirements, and physical force to prevent African Americans from voting.

1920 – The 19th Amendment

On August 18, 1920, Harry Burn, a young Tennessee representative from a mountain county changed his vote in the Tennessee legislature. The legislature had deadlocked over the ratification of the 19th Amendment to the Constitution extending the right to vote to women. The young man was fulfilling a promise he had made to his suffragette mother. His vote made Tennessee the 38th state to ratify the amendment which thus became the law of the land. Women had been organizing and fighting for the right to vote for 80 years. Some states had even allowed women to vote in local elections. This amendment made women's suffrage universal throughout the country.

The Right to Vote *(cont.)*

The Impact of Women's Suffrage

The entire nature of presidential elections was permanently changed as it always is when a group of people is enfranchised (given the right to vote). The 1916 presidential election had a total of over 17 million popular votes. The 1920 election had over 25 million votes. By 1928 the total jumped to over 35 million votes. Much more important was the steady influence of women on issues as diverse as war and peace, public safety, women's opportunity in the workplace, and issues dealing with the welfare of children and education.

The Voting Rights Act of 1965

The Civil Rights Movement of the 1950s and 1960s gradually forced a greater degree of equality for African Americans and people of other ethnic groups who faced racial restrictions. In 1964 the 24th Amendment to the Constitution outlawed poll taxes which had been used in several Southern states to restrict voting by poor African Americans and some whites as well.

The Voting Rights Act of 1965 allowed the federal government to prohibit states from preventing African Americans from voting. The government could intervene if fewer than half of the states' eligible African-American citizens had been registered. The law outlawed tests to determine voter eligibility, and it allowed federal examiners to register voters. Within a few years, African-American citizens throughout the South were registering, voting, and running successfully for public office.

The 26th Amendment

The Constitution had set 21 as the minimum age for voting. In the 1960s as the Vietnam War claimed the lives of thousands of young American soldiers, pressure built to reduce the age limit to 18. People felt that if these young people could fight and die for their country, they should have a voice in electing its leaders. This became the law of the land when the 26th Amendment passed in 1971.

Today

Today, with a population of more than 280 million Americans, about 200 million are eligible to vote. This is about 70% of the population. About 140 million are registered to vote.

General requirements for voting today are the following:

- You must be a citizen of the United States by birth or naturalization.
- You must be 18 or older.
- You must register to vote.
- You may not be convicted of a crime.

Democracy

What Is Democracy?

Democracy is the belief that people are capable of governing themselves. Democratic societies are committed to the idea that all members of a society have inherent human rights to life and liberty. Our American democracy evolved from the exercise of political power by the American colonists in managing their own affairs. When Great Britain tried to interrupt this local control and impose the authority of the King of England, the colonists revolted and set up their own government.

What Is Tyranny?

Governments which are under the complete control of a dictator, an absolute monarch (king), or a small group of all-powerful men are called dictatorships or tyrannies. In these governments, the rights of individuals are not considered important, and peoples' freedom to act is limited by a dictatorship. Individual hopes and personal desires are subjected to the overriding interest of the group in control. Communist dictatorships in the former Soviet Union and in China are examples of absolute rule by a small minority.

How Democracy Works

The Founding Fathers who wrote the Constitution designed a government that allows people to govern themselves. They did not believe that people had to make every law or decision themselves. They believed that people should have the right to select their own leaders who would make acceptable laws and appropriate decisions. Many of the founders believed that only the wealthy and respected white men in a community should have the right to vote for their leaders, but the system they created gradually expanded the right to vote to include virtually all adult citizens.

Checks and Balances

The men who wrote the Constitution feared excessive government and distrusted the human ambitions of many people. Therefore, they created a system of government at the federal level in which laws were made in one branch of government (the legislative) but enforced by another branch (the executive). A third branch (the judicial) could monitor the actions and laws created by the other two branches. In addition, the founders specified that many rights were reserved only to the states or the people and not to the federal government at all.

Democracy *(cont.)*

Evolution of Democracy

Many tribes of primitive peoples were run on democratic principles. The leaders of many American Indian tribes were selected by the tribe. Tribal decisions were often made in councils attended by the entire community. The development of settled agricultural communities and larger warrior tribes in Europe and Asia led to the rise of powerful kings. Occasional efforts were made to curb the powers of these leaders in ancient Greece, for example, and in medieval England. Modern democracy began to evolve with the American Revolution and later with the French Revolution. Powerful kings were often removed by popular uprisings. Sometimes this led to other dictatorships such as those in Russia and China.

Modern Democracy

Today, much of the modern world is governed by some form of democratic government. Some countries have kings (who often possess little real power), and representatives elected by the people make the laws. While dictatorships still exist in the world and often exercise fearsome power, the momentum for democracy is evident. Modern democratic governments not only have freely-elected officials but usually have economies where decisions are made by individuals and not the government. Businesses are free to buy and sell as they wish and to compete on equal terms. Although all governments exercise some control or regulation over certain industries such as electrical power, banking, and land ownership, most decisions are made by consumers in a democracy.

Making a Democracy Work

Successful democracies work effectively when individual citizens are able to do these things:

- Accept the will of the majority. Election outcomes must be respected and all groups need to cooperate in the process of making laws.

- Protect the rights of the minority. No laws can be acceptable which limit the freedoms of any one group of citizens.

- Obey all laws. No group can receive special favors or be exempt from obeying laws.

- Get involved in the process. Join groups that help to create meaningful change. Exercise the right to speak out on issues.

- Vote. Citizens who don't vote don't have a voice in their government.

Reading Comprehension Quiz

Electing a President

Directions: Read pages 7 and 8 about electing a president. Answer these questions based on the information in the selection. Circle the correct answer in each question below. Underline the sentence in the selection where the answer is found.

1. Where is the first presidential caucus held?
   - A. New Hampshire
   - B. Iowa
   - C. California
   - D. Ohio

2. A candidate's team may help him do which of the following?
   - A. raise money
   - B. talk to the press
   - C. both A and B
   - D. work in the electoral college

3. When is the new president inaugurated?
   - A. January
   - B. August
   - C. September
   - D. February

4. For about how long does the official presidential campaign last?
   - A. two months
   - B. one year
   - C. four years
   - D. six months

5. Which election makes the actual determination of a president's election?
   - A. primary election
   - B. electoral college election
   - C. caucus
   - D. nominating convention

6. In what month are presidential elections held?
   - A. November
   - B. September
   - C. January
   - D. October

7. Which modern presidential debate set a model for future debates?
   - A. Kennedy/Johnson
   - B. Lincoln/Douglas
   - C. Roosevelt/Taft
   - D. Kennedy/Nixon

8. Where is the first presidential primary held?
   - A. New York
   - B. Iowa
   - C. North Carolina
   - D. New Hampshire

9. Where is a presidential candidate formally selected by his party?
   - A. party caucus
   - B. primary election
   - C. national election
   - D. national convention

10. On what day of the week are national presidential elections held?
   - A. Sunday
   - B. Monday
   - C. Tuesday
   - D. Thursday

Reading Comprehension Quiz (cont.)

The History of Presidential Elections

Directions: Read pages 9 through 12 about the history of presidential elections. Answer these questions based on the information in the selection. Circle the correct answer in each question below. Underline the sentence in the selection where the answer is found.

1. Who was the only President of the United States elected without any major opposition?
   A. John Adams
   B. George Washington
   C. Thomas Jefferson
   D. John Kennedy

2. Which candidate received the same number of electoral ballots as Thomas Jefferson in the election of 1800?
   A. Aaron Burr
   B. John Adams
   C. Alexander Hamilton
   D. George Washington

3. Who was killed in a duel resulting from the election of 1800?
   A. Aaron Burr
   B. Alexander Hamilton
   C. John Adams
   D. Thomas Jefferson

4. Which president spent almost his entire presidency involved in a Civil War?
   A. Abraham Lincoln
   B. Theodore Roosevelt
   C. Harry Truman
   D. George Bush

5. Who received the most popular and electoral votes in the 1824 election but still lost the presidency?
   A. John Adams
   B. John Quincy Adams
   C. Andrew Jackson
   D. Henry Clay

6. Who won the most popular votes in the 1876 election?
   A. Rutherford B. Hayes
   B. Abraham Lincoln
   C. Samuel Tilden
   D. Theodore Roosevelt

7. Who was the presidential candidate of the Bull Moose Party?
   A. Theodore Roosevelt
   B. Franklin Roosevelt
   C. William Howard Taft
   D. Harry Truman

8. Who won more popular votes but fewer electoral votes than his opponent?
   A. George Washington
   B. George Bush
   C. Abraham Lincoln
   D. Al Gore

9. Which president was elected to four terms?
   A. Theodore Roosevelt
   B. George Washington
   C. Franklin Roosevelt
   D. John Kennedy

10. Which president had to resign because of the Watergate scandal?
    A. John Kennedy
    B. Richard Nixon
    C. Franklin Roosevelt
    D. Harry Truman

Reading Comprehension Quiz *(cont.)*

American Elections

Directions: Read pages 13 through 15 about American elections. Answer these questions based on the information in the selection. Circle the correct answer in each question below. Underline the sentence in the selection where the answer is found.

1. Which of these elective offices is in the federal government?
   A. governor
   B. United States senator
   C. mayor
   D. comptroller

2. Which of these elective offices is in the state government?
   A. president
   B. United States senator
   C. mayor
   D. comptroller

3. Approximateley how many state and local governments exist in the United States?
   A. 500,000
   B. 55,000
   C. 85,000
   D. 100

4. Which of these candidates has no party affiliation?
   A. Democratic
   B. nonpartisan
   C. Independent
   D. Republican

5. In which year will a presidential election be held?
   A. 2006
   B. 2005
   C. 2008
   D. 2007

6. How many U. S. senators are up for election in a federal election?
   A. one-third
   B. all 100
   C. none
   D. six

7. Who determines educational policy for local schools?
   A. school boards
   B. sanitation commissions
   C. U. S. senators
   D. city councils

8. Which of these elective offices is in the local government?
   A. attorney general
   B. congressman
   C. mayor
   D. comptroller

9. How many elected officials serve in some government in the United States?
   A. 85,000
   B. 500,000
   C. 3 million
   D. 100 million

10. Which of the following is a branch of the federal government?
    A. judicial
    B. executive
    C. commission
    D. both A and B

Reading Comprehension Quiz (cont.)

The Right to Vote

Directions: Read pages 16 and 17 about the right to vote. Answer these questions based on the information in the selection. Circle the correct answer in each question below. Underline the sentence in the selection where the answer is found.

1. Which amendment to the Constitution gave newly freed slaves the right to vote?
   A. 12th   C. 19th
   B. 15th   D. 26th

2. Which amendment to the Constitution outlawed the use of poll taxes?
   A. 24th   C. 15th
   B. 12th   D. 26th

3. How many Americans are eligible to vote today?
   A. 100 million   C. 200 million
   B. 140 million   D. 280 million

4. What does *enfranchised* mean?
   A. a business   C. the right to vote
   B. register   D. poll tax

5. What is the voting age in the United States today?
   A. 18   C. 16
   B. 21   D. 25

6. Which amendment to the Constitution gave women the right to vote?
   A. 24th   C. 19th
   B. 15th   D. 26th

7. Which state was the 38th state to ratify the 19th Amendment?
   A. New York   C. South Carolina
   B. Tennessee   D. California

8. What percentage of the population voted in the Lincoln election of 1860?
   A. 14%   C. 3%
   B. 7%   D. 70%

9. In order to vote, you must. . .
   A. attend college   C. drive a car
   B. pay a tax   D. register

10. What is the meaning of the word *suffrage*?
    A. suffer   C the right to vote
    B. anger   D. election

Reading Comprehension Quiz *(cont.)*

Democracy

Directions: Read pages 18 and 19 about democracy. Answer these questions based on the information in the selection. Circle the correct answer in each question below. Underline the sentence in the selection where the answer is found.

1. Which word means the belief that people are capable of self government?
   - A. democracy
   - B. tyranny
   - C. monarchy
   - D. dictatorship

2. Which branch of the federal government makes laws?
   - A. executive
   - B. legislative
   - C. judicial
   - D. FBI

3. Which revolution led to the evolution of modern democracy?
   - A. French
   - B. American
   - C. Russian
   - D. Chinese

4. In which of these governments are officials freely elected by the citizens?
   - A. absolute monarchy
   - B. tyranny
   - C. democracy
   - D. dictatorship

5. What is the name for a small group of all-powerful men in a government?
   - A. democracy
   - B. legislature
   - C. monarchy
   - D. dictatorship

6. Which of these governments believes that its citizens have inherent rights to liberty and life?
   - A. communist
   - B. absolute monarchy
   - C. democracy
   - D. dictatorship

7. Which branch of the federal government enforces the laws?
   - A. executive
   - B. legislative
   - C. judicial
   - D. courts

8. Who wrote the United States Constitution?
   - A. Congress
   - B. Founding Fathers
   - C. President Washington
   - D. Abraham Lincoln

9. Which of these phrases is closest in meaning to the word *minority*?
   - A. most of the voters
   - B. poor people
   - C. women
   - D. less than half of the voters

10. Which of these could be an absolute monarch?
    - A. President of the U. S.
    - B. king
    - C. congressman
    - D. governor

Teacher Lesson Plans

Reading Comprehension—Oral Language

Objective: Students will develop skills in oral presentation techniques in speech and debate.

Materials

- copies of You Are the Candidate (pages 27 and 28)

- copies of Giving a Speech (pages 29 and 30)

- copies of Great Presidential Debates (pages 31)

- copies of Your Presidential Debate (pages 32)

- copies of Class Election (pages 33)

- books, encyclopedias, and Internet sources

Procedures

1. Discuss presidential politics, review some current events, and discuss the incumbent president. Distribute You Are the Candidate (pages 27 and 28). Review the assignments and the issues listed. Explain that this is the initial step in a political campaign for each student. Monitor and critique student work in progress.

2. Distribute Giving a Speech (pages 29 and 30). Review the assignment for writing the speech in terms of length and relevant details. Discuss the techniques for effective public speaking. Monitor and critique student's written work. Encourage students to practice before their final presentations. Allocate class time for each student to deliver his or her speech.

3. Review the concept of presidential debates with your class. Distribute Great Presidential Debates (page 31). Review the research assignment and the written response to literature. Assign due dates and allocate computer time.

4. Review the concept of presidential debates. Distribute Your Presidential Debate (page 32). Review the format for the debate in your class. Plan to conduct debates with about five candidates at a time and panels of three or four student questioners. Review the procedures listed on page 32 and explain that you expect the debates to be conducted with a serious demeanor. Stress the importance of audience attention and involvement. Allocate time for the debates.

5. Distribute Class Election (page 33). Review the procedures for conducting the election. Encourage students to create the posters and commercials. Conduct the primary election to reduce the number of candidates to two final candidates. (Students may vote for two candidates in the primary election so they can vote for themselves and another candidate.) Conduct the final election.

Assessment—Have students share their feelings and experiences with the class. Keep an ongoing assessment record of each child's participation in the election process.

Teacher Lesson Plans *(cont.)*

Reading Comprehension—Written and Oral Language

Objective: Students will develop skills in persuasive writing and oral presentation techniques in speech.

Materials

- copies of Public Speaking (pages 34 and 35)
- copies of Take a Stand (pages 36–38)
- books, encyclopedias, and Internet sources

Procedures

1. Distribute Public Speaking (pages 34 and 35). Encourage students to select a famous speech or a portion of the speech to deliver. Monitor student progress and schedule class time for student speeches over a period of several days.

2. Distribute Take a Stand (pages 36–38). Review the format for a persuasive essay. Allow students ample time to complete the essay using the writing process.

Assessment—Have students share stories, speeches, and debates with the entire class. Encourage all students to critique their activities.

Reading Comprehension—Classroom Literature

Objective: Students will become acquainted with the humorous and serious books of Robert Newton Peck.

Materials

- copies of *Soup for President* (pages 39 and 40)
- copies of Focus on the Author: Robert Newton Peck (page 41)
- copies of Robert Newton Peck – The Books (page 42)
- copies of Reading Inventory (page 43)

Procedure

1. Reproduce and distribute *Soup for President* (pages 39 and 40). Read and discuss the pages with the class. Have students read the book. Conduct literature circles or a full class discussion of the book. Use the discussion questions to stimulate student interest and to assess comprehension. If copies are difficult to obtain, use the book as a read-aloud.

2. Reproduce and distribute Focus on the Author: Robert Newton Peck (page 41). Have students read the page. Then conduct a class discussion about the author's life and work.

3. Reproduce and distribute Robert Newton – The Books (page 42). Encourage students to read one of the titles by Robert Newton Peck and make a brief oral report to the class detailing the highlights of the book. They could use the Reading Inventory (page 43) as the basis of the report.

Assessment—Have students share oral reports with the class and participate in general class discussions. Use the discussion questions on page 39 as an assessment vehicle for student reading of *Soup for President*.

You Are the Candidate

- You are running for President of the United States in the next presidential election year.
- You are going to represent the people you feel have been ignored or whose concerns you support.
- You intend to conduct a campaign based on issues which are important to you.

Assignment

Make a list of every national issue you think is important. These issues might involve any of the topics listed below plus other matters of concern to you. Next to the issue indicate your positions, opinions, and solutions for dealing with the problem.

- war and peace in various parts of the world

- terrorism at home and abroad

- unemployment and job opportunities

- equal pay for equal work and worker rights

- treatment of women in the workplace

- minority rights and racial preferences

- taxes–who pays them and how much

- opportunities for young people

- medical care for the poor and the aging

- the economy

You Are the Candidate *(cont.)*

Assignment *(cont.)*

Your Issues　　　　　　　　　　　　　**Your Opinions and Solutions**

_____　　　_____

_____　　　_____

_____　　　_____

_____　　　_____

_____　　　_____

_____　　　_____

_____　　　_____

_____　　　_____

Setting Priorities

1. Study the issues you listed above.
2. Choose five issues that are the most important concerns to you.
3. Write a reason to explain why each of the five topics you selected is more important than the other issues.

Reasons

1. _____

   _____

2. _____

   _____

3. _____

   _____

4. _____

   _____

5. _____

   _____

Giving a Speech

Giving a Speech

Presidential candidates need to be skilled in holding the attention of an audience. They need to express themselves, clearly, forcefully, and effectively. Voters are not impressed by speakers with poor expression, inarticulate ideas, mumbling voices, or distracting habits.

Write a Campaign Speech

Use You Are the Candidate to cluster or pre-write for your campaign speech. Write a speech about three to four minutes long to deliver to your class. Focus especially on the key issues of your campaign.

Your speech should have:

- an opening paragraph stating your purpose
- four to six paragraphs expressing each of the main points in clear, logical, precise language
- a concluding paragraph which summarizes your thinking.

Refine Your Speech

Your speech will have a greater effect on your listeners if you use:

- anecdotes or stories to illustrate some of your main points
- evidence and facts to support each of your main points
- one or two brief quotations from experts to support your opinions
- an attention-getting opening sentence
- a sharply focused closing sentence.

Giving a Speech *(cont.)*

Delivering Your Speech

You may choose to memorize your speech and simply use your paper as back up in case you forget something. Another method is to use note cards and speak extemporaneously, in an impromptu manner, as if you were speaking to friends. In either style of speech, use these techniques to connect with your audience.

Good Posture – Stand straight. Balance your feet. Relax your body. Tell yourself to be comfortable. Center your mind.

Eye Contact – Look at various sections of the audience as you speak but not at any one person in particular.

Rehearse Out Loud – Give your speech out loud in full voice to a mirror, a friend, a sibling, or your parents. Practice several times.

Volume – Vary your voice pattern. Be conversational at times but speak more forcefully on important points. Never shout but always be loud enough to hear.

Breathe from Your Diaphragm – Take deep breaths between paragraphs and important points but don't be obvious about it. (The diaphragm is the large muscle at the bottom of your rib cage which allows you to control your breathing.)

Speak Slowly and Clearly – Speak a little slower than normal speech patterns. Don't race to get done.

Enjoy the Experience – Public speaking is a great accomplishment.

| 1750 | 1800 | 1850 | 1900 | 1950 | 2000 |

Great Presidential Debates

The Lincoln – Douglas debates are among the most famous debates in American history. The skill and passion of the two men helped to crystallize the issue of slavery for the nation. The Kennedy – Nixon debates reintroduced the idea of presidential debates to 20th century Americans. Debates have become a regular campaign feature of most presidential contests since 1976. More recently George W. Bush and Al Gore engaged in a series of debates which helped citizens to decide on their preferences in that presidential race. Debates are also held between candidates within a party. The Republican candidates of 2000 and the Democratic candidates of 2000 and 2004 have held party debates in an effort to win primary elections.

Internet Assignment

Use the Internet (or any other available sources—books, encyclopedias, or almanacs) to research information about any presidential debate.

Use the following guidelines to help you.

1. name of the debating candidates

2. year the debate was held

3. number of debates

4. length of time for each debate

5. at least three major issues debated

6. personal habits or quirks of the candidates

7. results of the debate(s)

Response to Research

Write an essay expressing your opinion about the value of presidential debates. Your essay should include the importance of the debates in forming opinions, the response of the voters, the value of the questions, the clarity of the candidates' responses, and any other concerns you have. Your essay should express clear reasoning, be based on the research you did, and be carefully edited. The essay should be three to five paragraphs in length.

1750　　　　1800　　　　1850　　　　1900　　　　1950　　　　2000

Your Presidential Debate

Debating is important because you learn how to take a position and defend it using all of the facts and evidence you can collect and organize into effective talking points. You are going to defend your positions and promote your candidacy in a presidential debate in your classroom.

Debate Format

Presidential debates have various formats. Your debate will have a panel of questioners acting as news correspondents or private citizens.

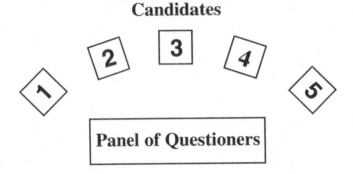

Candidates

Panel of Questioners

Introduction

- Each candidate will have two minutes to give an introductory speech explaining his or her candidacy and briefly describing the issues that concern the candidate.

Questions

- One questioner will ask a question of one candidate. The candidate will respond to the question.
- Each of the other candidates will have an opportunity to make a comment.
- The next questioner on the panel will ask a question and candidates will respond again.
- Every candidate will have the opportunity to be questioned twice.
- Every candidate will have the opportunity to comment on each question asked of any candidate.

One-on-One

- Each candidate is permitted to ask one question of another candidate.
- The other candidate responds.

Closing Arguments

- Each candidate has one minute to sum up his or her candidacy and to express any final thoughts.

Assignment

Using the information listed above as a guideline, do the following:

1. Prepare your opening speech (two minutes).
2. Make a list of possible questions you might be asked.
3. Prepare your responses to these questions.
4. Prepare your closing remarks (one minute).

Class Election

The Campaign

You have been running for president for some time. You've given speeches and participated in debates. Election time in class is drawing near. Spruce up your campaign with the following:

1. Make one or several posters advertising your candidacy. These posters could show your face or advertise your positions.
2. Make a brief video or tape recorded commercial promoting your run for the highest office in the land.
3. Convince one or several of your classmates to sign a statement of support for your candidacy.
4. Start a recess rally for your supporters with balloons, posters, and a brief speech.
5. Prepare a victory speech in case you win the final election.
6. Prepare a concession speech in case you lose.

The Primary Election

- Your teacher will conduct a classroom election to select the two candidates with the highest totals.
- Each student may vote for two names on his or her ballot.
- The votes will be counted and the two names with the highest totals will be determined.

The Final Election

- A final vote will be taken.
- Each voter may write only one name of the final two candidates.
- The winner is the person who receives the most votes.

Public Speaking

Great Speeches

One kind of public speaking involves memorizing all or part of a great speech by a famous person and delivering it to an audience. Sometimes parts of famous documents like the Preamble to the Constitution or the Introduction to the Declaration of Independence are used. Speakers may also choose a long speech in a play, called a soliloquy. Certain special parts of a book might also be used.

Assignment

1. Choose one of the suggested speeches listed on the next page or a similar speech.
2. Select a part of the speech or the entire speech if it is less than five minutes long.
3. Memorize the speech. Try to get the tone and emphasis that the original speaker might have used.
4. Use all of the public speaking suggestions detailed on pages 29 and 30.
5. Deliver your speech to the class.

Public Speaking *(cont.)*

Selections

You can find these on the Internet, in books of famous speeches, in encyclopedias, in books about the speaker, and/or in other sources.

- Abraham Lincoln's First Inaugural Address

- Abraham Lincoln's Second Inaugural Address

- The Gettysburg Address by Abraham Lincoln

- President Kennedy's Inaugural Address

- "I Have a Dream" by Martin Luther King

- Franklin D. Roosevelt's First Inaugural Address

- Frederick Douglass' "The Conscience of the Nation Must Be Roused"

- Winston Churchill's "We Shall Fight in the Fields and Streets"

- Winston Churchill's "Iron Curtain Speech"

- The Preamble and Declaration of Rights in The Declaration of Independence

- Hamlet's "To Be or Not to Be" Soliloquy

- Daniel Webster's Bunker Hill Oration

- Benjamin Franklin's Final Speech at the Constitutional Convention

- Ronald Reagan's "Challenger Disaster" Speech

- Patrick Henry's "Give Me Liberty or Give Me Death" Oration

- Sojourner Truth's "Ain't I a Woman?"

- Seneca Falls Convention's Declaration of the Rights of Women

- "All the World's a Stage" from Shakespeare's *As You Like It*

Take a Stand

Throughout American history citizens have heatedly discussed and debated the great issues of their times. They have often published letters and essays in newspapers and magazines expressing their views.

Persuasive Essay

Write a persuasive essay on one of the suggested topics listed below or on another subject about which you have strong opinions.

Your essay should have at least four paragraphs and be organized like this:

> 1. The opening paragraph must clearly express your opinion and indicate why the subject is important to you.
>
> 2. The second paragraph should describe all of the evidence you can think of to support your opinion—this could include personal experiences, the opinions of experts, and careful reasoning.
>
> 3. The third paragraph should describe the arguments and evidence against your position and your response and reactions to these arguments.
>
> 4. The concluding paragraph must briefly restate your position and clearly draw together all of the elements of your thinking.

Take a Stand *(cont.)*

Suggested Topics

- Should the electoral college be abolished?

- Should the President of the United States be elected to one six-year term?

- Should every American be entitled to health care?

- Should national elections be held on a Saturday or Sunday instead of Tuesday?

- Should every adult American be entitled to a job?

- Should the United States have gone to war in Iraq?

- The greatest President of the United States was . . .

- Should the President of the United States have to receive a Declaration of War from Congress before sending troops into any conflict?

- Should African Americans be paid reparations for slavery in early America?

- Should some students receive preferential admissions to colleges because they come from disadvantaged communities?

Take a Stand *(cont.)*

Pre-write

Do your pre-write planning or cluster here.

Title _____

1. your opinion/importance of the subject	2. the evidence and your experiences
3. arguments against/for your response	4. concluding statement

| 1750 | 1800 | 1850 | 1900 | 1950 | 2000 |

Soup for President

Soup for President by Robert Newton Peck is an exciting story with a great deal of humor and a touch of history. Set in the Depression-era years of the 1930s, *Soup for President* records the escapades of two boys in rural Vermont determined to elect Soup as the class president. The main character, narrator, and author of the book is Robert Newton Peck. The title character is Soup, an ambitious leader with lots of imagination and misdirected energy. Norma Jean is the other candidate for president who offers Robert an unusual bribe to support her.

Assignment

1. Read *Soup for President*. Read at least two chapters a day.
2. Respond to the discussion questions below.
3. Complete the character sketches on page 40.

Discussion Questions

1. Why do you think Soup and Norma Jean decide to run for class president?

2. Why did Miss Kelly tell Rob that he was chivalrous?

3. How do the boys feel about their teacher, Miss Kelly?

4. Who seems to do most of the work in their adventures—Soup or Rob?

5. Who changed her vote so that Soup won? Why did she do it?

6. Why did Rob sing under Norma Jean's window? Why did he choose the song he sang?

7. Why did Miss Kelly want the boys to remove Soup's name from the barn?

8. Should Rob have taken the ruler or read the note?

9. What national election is going on at the same time?

Soup for President (cont.)

Character Sketches

Write a brief cluster of words or phrases to describe each of the characters named here.

Soup	Rob
Norma Jean	**Miss Kelly**

Focus on the Author: Robert Newton Peck

Robert Newton Peck writes funny books. The Soup series (listed on page 42) contains some of the most hilarious stories in all of children's literature. Whether it's using a young sapling to whip apples through the window of the Baptist Church, crashing into a Halloween party riding a runaway wheelbarrow, losing all of their clothes in a skinny-dipping escapade, or arriving at a Christmas party in an airborne sleigh, Soup and Rob find tons of trouble and readers get loads of laughter.

Robert Newton Peck was born on February 17, 1928, on a Vermont farm near Lake Champlain. He grew up in the Depression years of the 1930s when nearly a third of the working men in the nation couldn't find work, many people were without homes and food, and President Franklin Roosevelt had been elected to get the country back to better economic times.

Robert Peck was brought up in the unique religious tradition of the Shakers who put great value on the simple life. His father was a butcher and farmer, but the family struggled to survive. Peck attended a one-room schoolhouse in his elementary school years. This kind of school had children from first through the sixth grades in the same room. Most of the students were the sons and daughters of uneducated farmers, lumbermen, and working men. It was here that Robert met the real Miss Kelly who clearly had an enormous impact on his life.

Robert's father died when he was young, and Robert became the man of the house. He left school about the age of 12 and went to work doing whatever jobs he could find as a lumberman, hog butcher, and paper mill worker. He was needed to care for his mother, his aunt, and the family home and farm. The story of his early life is told from a humorous perspective in the Soup books. Rob's free spirit, fondness for adventure, and personal friendships offer one aspect of his youth. The serious side of Peck's youth is portrayed in his first book entitled *A Day No Pigs Would Die*. This autobiography, written in less than three weeks when Peck was 45, was his first book. *A Day No Pigs Would Die* describes the loss of his father and Peck's struggle to support his family.

Peck joined the army at the age of 17 and fought in World War II as an infantryman. After the war, he entered college and graduated in 1953, despite the fact that he had not had a high school education. He worked in advertising and married in 1958.

His best man at the wedding was his good friend, Fred Rogers, of television fame. Peck has two children. Peck began writing in 1973. Remarkably, his first book, *A Day No Pigs Would Die*, was an instant success, and he has been writing ever since.

Robert Newton Peck – The Books

Listed here is a selected bibliography of books by Robert Newton Peck.

Soup Series

Soup. Knopf, 1998.

Soup for President. Knopf, 1998.

Soup in the Saddle. Knopf, 1988.

Soup's Goat. Knopf, 1987.

Soup in Love. Dell, 1992.

Soup's Hoop. Dell, 1992.

Soup and Me. Knopf, 1975.

Soup's Drum. Knopf, 1980.

Soup on Wheels. Knopf, 1981.

Soup on Ice. Knopf, 1985.

Soup 1776. Knopf, 1995.

Soup's Uncle. Dell, 1990.

Other Titles

A Day No Pigs Would Die. Knopf, 1972.

Secrets of Successful Fiction. Writer's Digest, 1980.

Eagle Fur. Thorndike, 1992.

A Part of the Sky. Knopf, 1994.

Arly. Walker, 1991.

Reading Inventory

Assignment

Read one of the books listed on the previous page. Complete the questions below.

1. Write a brief outline of the plot of the story in a few sentences.

   _____

   _____

   _____

2. List the major characters.

   _____

   _____

   _____

3. Write a brief sketch of one character.

   _____

   _____

   _____

4. Is the story written in the first person (I) or the third person (he, she, they)?

   _____

   _____

   _____

5. Which character do you like best? Explain.

   _____

   _____

   _____

6. Describe your favorite incident that happened in the story.

   _____

   _____

   _____

Teacher Lesson Plans

Reading Comprehension—Working with Timelines

Objectives: Students will learn to derive information from a timeline and make timelines relevant to them.

Materials

- copies of Presidential Elections Timeline (page 46)
- research resources including books, encyclopedias, texts, atlases, almanacs, and Internet sites

Procedure

1. Collect all available resources for your students so that they have plenty of places to find information.
2. Reproduce and distribute the Presidential Elections Timeline (page 46) activity sheet. Review the concept of a timeline, possibly using the school year as an example.
3. Review the various events listed on the timeline.
4. Assign students to find additional dates for the timeline as described in the assignment on page 46.
5. Students may want to use the readings from previous lessons to locate additional dates for their timelines.
6. Have students create their own personal timelines as described in the assignment at the bottom of page 46.

Assessment—Share additions to the timeline in a classroom discussion using a board or chart to list the new dates. Have students share their personal timelines in small groups.

Reading Comprehension—Working with Maps

Objective: Students will learn to use and derive information from a variety of map forms.

Materials

- copies of Electoral Map of the United States – 2004 Election (page 47)
- copies of Electoral Math (pages 48–50)
- copies of Bush – Gore 2000 (pages 51 and 52)
- atlases, almanacs, and other maps for reference and comparison

Procedure

1. Review the map on page 47. Have the students use the information on the page to complete the activities on pages 48–50. Have students use the suggested sources to complete the page.
2. Review the map on page 51 entitled Bush – Gore 2000. Point out that the shaded states represent Gore's electoral votes and the unshaded votes. Have students complete the assignment on page 52.

Assessment—Correct the activity pages with the students. Check for understanding and review basic concepts.

Teacher Lesson Plans *(cont.)*

Reading Comprehension—Famous People Research

Objective: Students will develop skills in finding, organizing, and presenting research information.

Materials

- copies of Become a President of the United States (pages 53–57)
- copies of Presidents of the United States (page 58)
- books, encyclopedias, and Internet sources

Procedure

1. Review the information on Become a President of the United States (pages 53–57). Stress organizing materials, studying notes, and practicing techniques for presentation.
2. Review the research guidelines. Encourage students to select presidents or first ladies about whom a great deal has been written. Explain that facts don't need to be found in the order shown on the guidelines, but students should find almost every topic listed.
3. Review list of potential presidents and first ladies on the Presidents of the United States (page 58) activity sheet. Explain that first ladies should be very knowledgeable about their husbands career and presidential service.
4. Allow students time to prepare their research-based presentations. Then, arrange a schedule of presentations.

Assessment—Assess students on the basis of their written notes and oral classroom presentations.

1750	1800	1850	1900	1950	2000

Presidential Elections Timeline

1787	The presidency is conceived at the Constitutional Convention by the founding fathers.
1789	George Washington is elected president.
1800	Thomas Jefferson is elected after receiving 36 votes in the House of Representatives.
1824	John Quincy Adams defeats Andrew Jackson for the presidency in the House of Representatives.
1828	Frontier hero Andrew Jackson wins the presidency.
1832	National party conventions are held for the first time.
1860	Abraham Lincoln is elected president in a four-way contest that leads to the Civil War.
1865	Abraham Lincoln is assassinated as the Civil War ends.
1869	The 15th Amendment grants African Americans the right to vote.
1876	Rutherford B. Hayes is chosen president by an electoral commission despite having fewer popular votes than his opponent.
1888	President Benjamin Harrison is elected with about 100,000 fewer popular votes than Grover Cleveland.
1912	Teddy Roosevelt fails to win election on the Bull Moose ticket.
1920	The 19th Amendment gives women the right to vote.
1932	Franklin Roosevelt wins the first of four consecutive elections as president.
1948	Harry Truman wins upset victory over Thomas Dewey.
1960	John F. Kennedy wins very close victory over Richard Nixon.
1965	The Voting Rights Act is passed.
1971	The 26th Amendment is passed lowering voting age to 18.
1972	President Nixon is reelected in an election marred by the Watergate scandal.
2000	George W. Bush wins an extremely close election.

Assignment

1. Study the timeline above.

2. Find at least 10 dates in American History to add to the timeline. They may go before, during, or after the timeline. These dates could include wars, inventions, other presidential elections, disasters, or sporting events among many other events. Make a list of these dates in chronological (time) order to share with the class. Be sure you know a little background information about each of your additional dates.

3. Create a timeline of your personal lifetime since the year you were born. Include the important events of your life. Then add events that happened in your country or the world during the same time. These events could include terrorist attacks, wars, presidential elections, important people who died, sporting events, earthquakes, floods, or happenings in popular culture.

Electoral Map of the United States (2004 Election)

The number of votes each state has in the electoral college is determined by the population of the state. The census, taken every 10 years, tells which states have grown or shrunk in population as a percentage of the nation, and electoral adjustments are taken after each census. In the last census, some states, such as New York and Pennsylvania, lost votes. Other states, such as Texas and California, gained votes.

The number of electoral votes in a state is equal to the number of U. S. Senators (two) plus the number of representatives in the House of Representatives. The number of representatives varies from one in states with small populations like Wyoming to 55 in California. Therefore, no state has fewer than three electoral votes. (The District of Columbia is not a state. It has three electoral votes but no senators or members of Congress.)

This map shows the number of electoral votes in each state.

Electoral Math

1. Study the map on the previous page.
2. List the number of electorial votes for each of these states? _____

California _____

Texas _____

Kansas _____

South Dakota_____

Florida _____

New Hampshire_____

Iowa _____

Vermont_____

Nevada _____

Mississippi_____

New York _____

Pennsylvania_____

North Carolina _____

Washington _____

New Mexico _____

Nebraska _____

Montana _____

Georgia _____

Alabama _____

Idaho _____

Electoral Math *(cont.)*

Directions

1. Study the electoral map on page 47.

2. Which state has the most electoral votes? _____

3. Which states, in addition to the District of Columbia, have only three electoral votes—the fewest any state can have?

   _____   _____   _____

   _____   _____   _____

   _____

4. It takes 270 electoral votes to elect a president. What is the fewest number of states it would take to elect a president? _____

   Name the states.

   _____   _____   _____

   _____   _____   Total votes:_____

   _____   _____

   _____   _____

   _____   _____

   _____

5. How many electoral votes does your state have? _____

6. How many members of the House of Representatives does your state have? _____

Electoral Math *(cont.)*

Compute the number of electoral votes in the 25 states with the least electoral votes plus the District of Columbia.

List the states, their electoral count, and the total below.

_____	_____	_____
_____	_____	_____
_____	_____	_____
_____	_____	_____
_____	_____	_____
_____	_____	_____
_____	_____	_____
_____	_____	_____
_____	_____	

Total votes: _____

Choose 20 states in which your presidential candidate wins all of the electoral votes. Name the states, list the electoral votes, and calculate the total vote.

_____	_____	_____
_____	_____	_____
_____	_____	_____
_____	_____	_____
_____	_____	_____
_____	_____	_____
_____	_____	

Total votes: _____

| 1750 | 1800 | 1850 | 1900 | 1950 | 2000 |

Bush – Gore 2000

Below is an electoral map of the Bush – Gore election in 2000.

The electoral count in some states is slightly different than on the map on page 47 which shows the electoral count for 2004 and 2008.

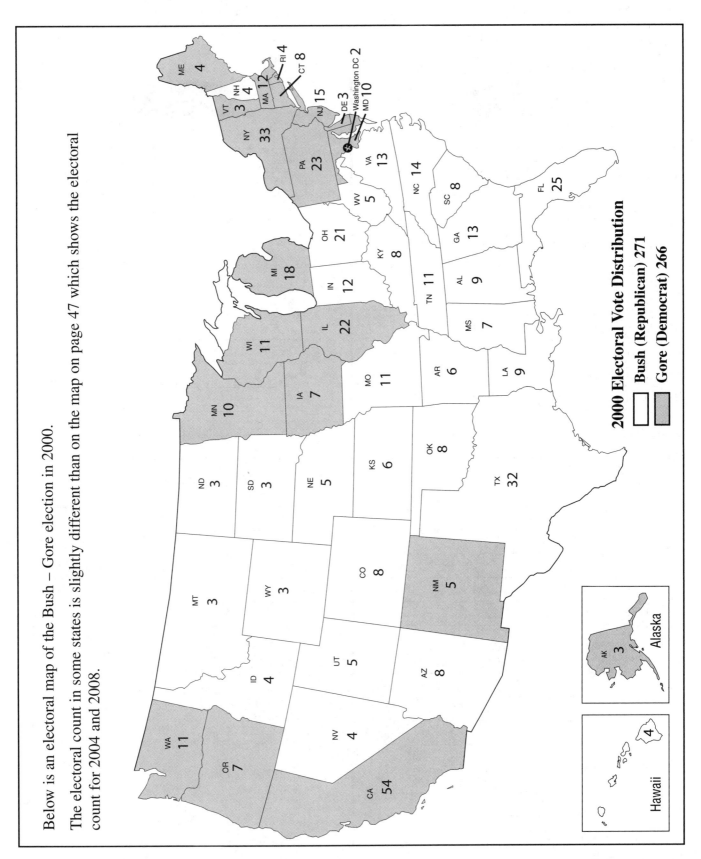

ME 4
RI 4
CT 8
NH 4
VT 3
MA 12
NY 33
NJ 15
PA 23
DE 3
Washington DC 2
MD 10
VA 13
WV 5
OH 21
KY 8
NC 14
SC 8
GA 13
FL 25
MI 18
IN 12
TN 11
AL 9
WI 11
IL 22
MS 7
MO 11
AR 6
LA 9
MN 10
IA 7
ND 3
SD 3
NE 5
KS 6
OK 8
TX 32
MT 3
WY 3
CO 8
NM 5
ID 4
UT 5
AZ 8
WA 11
OR 7
NV 4
CA 54
AK 3
Alaska
Hawaii 4

2000 Electoral Vote Distribution

☐ Bush (Republican) 271
▨ Gore (Democrat) 266

Bush – Gore 2000 *(cont.)*

Assignment

Study the electoral map on the previous page.

List all of the states and the electoral votes won by each candidate.

Bush

_____
_____
_____
_____
_____
_____
_____
_____
_____
_____
_____
_____
_____
_____
_____
_____
_____
_____
_____
_____
_____
_____
_____
_____
_____

Total Votes _____

Gore

_____
_____
_____
_____
_____
_____
_____
_____
_____
_____
_____
_____
_____
_____
_____
_____
_____
_____

Total Votes _____

Become a President of the United States

A great way to really understand presidential history is to become a President of the United States. Select a president and become familiar not only with the person but the times in which he lived. You will understand the issues of the era and acquire a sense of the day-to-day lifestyle of your President of the United States.

Select a President

Choose a President of the United States from the list on (page 58). Read enough about the president to make sure that he is someone who interests you and who will hold your attention. Before you finalize your choice, make sure that you can find several books in the library and information on the Internet about your president as well as Internet Websites.

Even though all of the presidents have been male, some girls may feel comfortable adopting the role of a president. Other girls may choose to be a first lady. The first lady should know all of the important facts about her husband's presidency as well as her own life.

Do the Research

Use the research model on the next two pages to find out everything you can about the president or first lady. Know the important dates, the vital statistics, the personal life, and the struggles of your president. Become familiar with your person's accomplishments. Begin to think of yourself as president or first lady. Try to assume the attitude and the personality of your chosen person.

Become a President of the United States *(cont.)*

Go to the Sources

- Use encyclopedias, almanacs, biographies, the Internet, and other sources of information to acquire the basic facts you need.

- You should find and use at least two full-length biographies about your president. You can also use adult biographies to research material not available in children's books.

- Use the index and table of contents of an adult biography to target specific information you need to know.

Take Careful Notes

- Use your own words.
- Write your facts clearly and briefly.
- Write down the basic facts in an orderly way. (The outline on pages 56 and 57 shows a good format to use.)
- Look for anecdotes and funny stories about your president.
- Study the notes.
- Get a friend to quiz you about your person so that you know what you need to study and are confident about what you know.
- When other students are being questioned, write down questions you couldn't answer about your own person and look the answers up later.

Become a President of the United States *(cont.)*

Get in Costume

- Put together an appropriate costume. Check your closets at home for slacks, shirts, or dress coats which might work. Check with parents, grandparents, older siblings, and friends for articles of clothing that might help. Ask for help getting to thrift stores for the missing pieces.
- Don't wear tennis shoes. Wear leather shoes. If they're too big, stuff them with tissue before putting them on for your presentation.

Be Famous

"My name is _____. What would you like to know about me?"

This is one way to begin your presentation. You might also want to give a brief presentation listing five or six important facts about your president. This will give your classmates a place to begin with their questions. Have a story to tell or something else to say if there is a momentary lull in the questioning.

Stay in Character

Don't forget who you are. You are a President of the United States—not another student in the class. Be very serious. Avoid any silly behaviors. At the end of the questions, review the important facts about your life.

Be Dramatic

- Use a loud voice. Don't drop your voice at the end of sentences.

- Use gestures. Use your arms and props to emphasize your points.

- Take charge of the classroom. Stride across the front.

- Be forceful, assertive, and self-assured.

- Have faith in yourself.

Organize Information

Use the guidelines on pages 56 and 57 to help you find and organize the information about your president.

Become a President of the United States *(cont.)*

Research Guidelines

I. Youth

A. Birthplace and date

B. Home life and experiences
   1. Siblings (brothers and sisters)
   2. Places lived (parts of the country) (farm or town)
   3. Circumstances (rich or poor) (important events to you)
   4. Age when you left home
   5. Parents (names and a fact or two)
   6. Activities and hobbies during childhood

C. Schooling (when?) (how much?)

D. Childhood heroes

E. Interesting facts and stories about your youth

II. Adult Life

A. Adventures and experiences
   1. Give details of each adventure or experience
   2. Places you traveled
   3. Fights and wars
   4. Dangers you faced

B. Lifestyle and personal habits
   1. Personal attitude toward life (list examples)
   2. Values you believe in
   3. Were you a risk-taker or cautious? (give examples)
   4. Personal behavior (cruel, kind, honest, etc.)
   5. Leadership experiences (Did men follow you? Why?)
   6. Physical abilities and disabilities (illnesses)

C. Personal information
   1. Marriage/children
   2. Jobs held
   3. Adult hobbies and interests

D. Reasons for fame
   1. Firsts (anything you did first as president)
   2. Inventions and discoveries (give complete details)
   3. Accomplishments (name and describe successes)
   4. Failures and things you didn't complete
   5. Greatest challenges you faced (describe and explain)

56

Become a President of the United States *(cont.)*

Research Guidelines *(cont.)*

III. End of Life

A. Death

   1. Date of death/age/cause of death

   2. Last words spoken (if known)

   3. Epitaph (words on tombstone, if any)

   4. Were you admired or forgotten by the time of your death?

IV. The Life and Times

A. Contemporaries

   1. Other famous people alive during your person's lifetime

   2. Presidents and public leaders of the time

B. Inventions and discoveries

   1. Important inventions of the time period

   2. Discoveries in medicine, science, or exploration

C. Travel and transportation (how people traveled)

D. Important events

   1. Wars and conflicts of the time

   2. Disasters (earthquakes, depressions, crashes, etc.)

V. Personal Evaluation

A. Admirable qualities

B. Unpleasant behaviors and prejudices

C. How you feel about your person

D. Questions you would ask your person if you could

E. Would you trust this person in your home? (reasons)

Presidents of the United States

	President	Dates Served	First Lady
1.	George Washington	1789–1797	Martha Washington
2.	John Adams	1797–1801	Abigail Adams
3.	Thomas Jefferson	1801–1809	Martha Jefferson
4.	James Madison	1809–1817	"Dolley" Madison
5.	James Monroe	1817–1825	Elizabeth Monroe
6.	John Quincy Adams	1825–1829	Louisa Adams
7.	Andrew Jackson	1829–1837	Rachel Jackson
8.	Martin Van Buren	1837–1841	Hannah Van Buren
9.	William H. Harrison	1841–1841	Anna Harrison
10.	John Tyler	1841–1845	Letitia Tyler
			Julia Tyler
11.	James Polk	1845–1849	Sarah Polk
12.	Zachary Taylor	1849–1850	Margaret Taylor
13.	Millard Fillmore	1850–1853	Abigail Fillmore
			Caroline Fillmore
14.	Franklin Pierce	1853–1857	Jane Pierce
15.	James Buchanan	1857–1861	(never married)
16.	Abraham Lincoln	1861–1865	Mary Lincoln
17.	Andrew Johnson	1865–1869	Eliza Johnson
18.	Ulysses S. Grant	1869–1877	Julia Grant
19.	Rutherford B. Hayes	1877–1881	Lucy Hayes
20.	James Garfield	1881–1881	Lucretia Garfield
21.	Chester A. Arthur	1881–1885	Ellen Arthur
22.	Grover Cleveland	1885–1889	Frances Cleveland
23.	Benjamin Harrison	1889–1893	Caroline Harrison
			Mary Harrison
24.	Grover Cleveland	1893–1897	Frances Cleveland
25.	William McKinley	1897–1901	Ida McKinley
26.	Theodore Roosevelt	1901–1909	Alice Roosevelt
			Edith Roosevelt
27.	William Howard Taft	1909–1913	Helen Taft
28.	Woodrow Wilson	1913–1921	Ellen Wilson
			Edith Wilson
29.	Warren Harding	1921–1923	Florence Harding
30.	Calvin Coolidge	1923–1929	Grace Coolidge
31.	Herbert Hoover	1929–1933	Lou Hoover
32.	Franklin Roosevelt	1933–1945	Eleanor Roosevelt
33.	Harry Truman	1945–1953	"Bess" Truman
34.	Dwight Eisenhower	1953–1961	Mamie Eisenhower
35.	John F. Kennedy	1961–1963	Jacqueline Kennedy
36.	Lyndon Johnson	1963–1969	"Lady Bird" Johnson
37.	Richard Nixon	1969–1974	"Pat" Nixon
38.	Gerald Ford	1974–1977	"Betty" Ford
39.	Jimmy Carter	1977–1981	Rosalyn Carter
40.	Ronald Reagan	1981–1989	"Nancy" Reagan
41.	George Bush	1989–1993	Barbara Bush
42.	Bill Clinton	1993–2001	Hillary Clinton
43.	George W. Bush	2001–	Laura Bush

1750 **1800** **1850** **1900** **1950** **2000**

Culminating Activities

Election Day

Set aside one day to be devoted to activities related to your study of presidential elections and democracy. You may choose to conduct your classroom election (page 33) as a part of this culminating activity. Encourage each of your students to come dressed as a president or first lady using costumes students wore during their research activity.

Parent Help

Encourage as many parents or older siblings as you can to come for all or part of the day to enjoy the proceedings and to help set up and monitor the activities. This is truly a day involving the family in the educational process. It helps to survey parents to discover any special talents, interests, or hobbies that would be a match for specific centers.

Format

You may choose to organize this day in a series of centers or as a series of whole class activities with a definite time allocated for each activity. If you do centers, the class is divided into groups with about six or seven students in each group. Each center should take about 20 to 30 minutes. Students then rotate to the next activity. Post the rotation schedule so students know when to move to the next center.

Presidential Convocation

Presidents and first ladies in this activity would make charts listing the central problems they faced in two categories: personal and national.

Speech

Students in this activity would reprise the speeches they wrote or the famous speeches they delivered. Students could also be given a topic for this activity and given 20 minutes to prepare a brief extemporaneous speech on the topic. Topics could include those listed on the next page:

Culminating Activities (cont.)

Speech (cont.)

- The most important problem facing America is . . .
- The greatest invention in history was . . .
- You should vote because . . .
- The greatest president was . . .
- The solution to the problem of homelessness is . . .
- Students should be able to drive at age 14 because . . .
- Schools should teach . . .

Map Making

A variety of maps could be created during this activity. Use the map section of this book for examples and find others in atlases, encyclopedias, and the Internet. Electoral maps and maps of the United States would usually be done by small teams of two or three students. Maps could be drawn on tagboard, large construction paper, or built in three-dimensional form using clay or salt and flour.

Debate and Discussion Activities

Several activities could be used where students would formally present the debates they participated in as presidential candidates.

Literature Activity

If your children read *Soup for President* together, you can set up an activity to have them react to the selection. They could take the parts of various characters or simply choose to read a book about the same subject or by the same author as a quiet break from the busy activities. Some possible selections are included in Robert Newton Peck – The Books (page 42).

Election Luncheon

If you have parent volunteers, plan a luncheon with an election theme. Parents and students could do the decorations together. A barbecue works well as a part of this theme.

1750   1800   1850   1900   1950   2000

Annotated Bibliography

Barber, James and Amy Pastan. *Smithsonian Presidents and First Ladies*. DK Publishing, 2002. (brief but interesting sketches of each president and his wife)

Davis, Kenneth C. *Don't Know Much About the Presidents*. HarperCollins, 2002. (interesting facts and anecdotes about the presidents)

Davis, Todd and Marc Frey. *The New Big Book of U. S. Presidents: Fascinating Facts about Each and Every President*. Running Book Press, 2001. (clever and anecdotal overviews of the presidents)

Dumbeck, Kristina. *Leaders of Women's Suffrage*. Lucent, 2001. (excellent overview of the suffrage movement and its leaders)

Feinberg, Barbara Silberdick. *Local Governments*. Franklin Watts, 1993. (excellent survey of various types of local governments)

Giesecke, Ernestine. *Governments Around the World*. Heinemann Library, 2000. (simple review of basic types of government)

Hargrove, Jim. *The Story of Presidential Elections*. Children's Press, 1988. (simple overview of significant presidential contests)

Henry, Christopher. *The Electoral College*. Franklin Watts, 1996. (good introduction to the origins and working of the Electoral College)

Isler, Claudia. *Individual Rights and Civic Responsibility: The Right to Vote*. Rosen, 2001. (full review of the development of the right to vote for women and minorities)

Maestro, Betsy and Maestro, Giulio. *The Voice of the People: American Democracy in Action*. Lothrop, Lee and Shepard, 1996. (easy text and simple survey of the branches of government)

Monroe, Judy. *The Nineteenth Amendment: Women's Right to Vote*. Enslow, 1998. (solid account of the effort to pass the women's suffrage amendment)

Pascoe, Elaine. *The Right to Vote*. Millbrook, 1997. (succinct survey of evolution of voting rights)

Provensen, Alice. *The Buck Stops Here: The Presidents of the United States*. HarcourtBrace & Co., 1997. (well-illustrated chart format with brief highlights of each presidency)

Shuker-Haines, Frances. *Rights and Responsibilities: Using Your Freedom*. Steck-Vaughn, 1993. (basic overview of rights and responsibilities of American citizenship)

Skarmeas, Nancy J. *First Ladies of the White House*. Ideals Publications, 2000. (good introduction to each first lady)

Steins, Richard. *Our Elections*. Millbrook, 1994. (good introduction to the history of presidential elections)

Sachar, Louis. *Class President*. Random House, 1999. (amusing account of a presidential visit to a classroom)

Garrison, Webb. *White House Ladies*. Rutledge Hill Press, 1996. (interesting anecdotes about each first lady)

The Annals of America. Encyclopedia Britannica, 1968. (reference work with every important American speech)

Glossary

amendment—a change to a legal document such as the Constitution

campaign—a candidate's plan and progress for an election

caucus—a party meeting to choose candidates

compromise—an agreement in which each side makes concessions

Constitution—the basic framework of laws in the United States

debate—a carefully prepared argument between individuals or teams

delegate—a person who represents others at a meeting

elector—an individual chosen by voters to vote for a specific candidate in the electoral college

electoral college—the group of persons elected by the people to elect the President of the United States

electoral votes—the votes a presidential candidate receives from the electoral college

executive—branch of government charged with enforcing laws

extemporaneous—speech with little apparent preparation

franchise—the right to vote

general election—an election held between candidates of different parties

legislative—the branch of government where the laws are written

literacy test—a reading or writing test used to discriminate against African American or poor white voters in some Southern states

majority—more than half of all votes cast

minority—less than half of a group

national convention—a meeting held by a party every four years to choose a presidential candidate

plurality—the highest total vote count among several candidates but totaling less than 50% of the vote

poll tax—a tax a citizen must pay before voting; used at one time in some Southern states to curtail voting by African Americans or poor whites

popular vote—the election totals of individual voters

President of the United States—the chief executive officer of the government of the United States

primary election—an election held to determine the candidates for each party before the general election

ratify—to officially approve

recall election—an election called to decide whether to remove an elected official

register—to sign up to vote

runoff election—an election between the two highest vote-getters in a previous election

senator—one of 100 members of the United States Senate

separation of powers—the division of government into three branches—legislative, executive, and judicial; to prevent tyranny or misuse of power

slate—a list of candidates, usually of one party

suffrage—the right to vote

suffragettes—women who advocated for their right to vote

turnout—the total number of voters in an election

Answer Key

Page 20

1. B
2. C
3. A
4. A
5. B
6. A
7. D
8. D
9. D
10. C

Page 21

1. B
2. A
3. B
4. A
5. C
6. C
7. A
8. D
9. C
10. B

Page 22

1. B
2. D
3. C
4. B
5. C
6. A
7. A
8. C
9. B
10. D

Page 23

1. B
2. A
3. C
4. C
5. A
6. C
7. B
8. A
9. D
10. C

Page 24

1. A
2. B
3. B
4. C
5. D
6. C
7. A
8. B
9. D
10. B

Page 39

1. Answers will vary.
2. Rob took the ruler punishment rather than read the note aloud.
3. They admire her.
4. Rob does the work. Soup does the directing.
5. Norma Jean. She thought the boys had worked hard to win.
6. Miss Kelly told the boys that she would want any prospective beau to serenade her. It was the romantic thing to do.

7. The owner was on the school board.
8. Answers will vary.
9. 1936 presidential election – Roosevelt vs. Landon

Page 48

California 55

New York 31

Texas 34

Pennsylvania 21

Kansas 6

North Carolina 15

South Dakota 3

Washington 11

Florida 27

New Mexico 5

New Hampshire 4

Nebraska 5

Iowa 7

Montana 3

Vermont 3

Georgia 15

Nevada 5

Alabama 9

Mississippi 6

Idaho 4

Page 49

2. California

3. Wyoming

   Montana

   Alaska

   North Dakota

   South Dakota

   Vermont

Answer Key *(cont.)*

Delaware

4. 11 states

California 55

Texas 3

New York 31

Florida 27

Illinois 21

Pennsylvania 21

Ohio 20

Michigan 17

Georgia 15

North Carolina 15

New Jersey 15

271 electoral votes

5. Answers will vary.

6. Answers will vary.

Page 50

District of Columbia 3

Wyoming 3

Montana 3

Alaska 3

North Dakota 3

South Dakota 3

Vermont 3

Delaware 3

Idaho 4

Hawaii 4

New Hampshire 4

Maine 4

Rhode Island 4

Nevada 5

Utah 5

New Mexico 5

Nebraska 5

West Virginia 5

Kansas 6

Arkansas 6

Mississippi 6

Oregon 7

Iowa 7

Oklahoma 7

South Carolina 8

Kentucky 8 or Connecticut 8

124 electoral votes

Page 52

Bush

Idaho 4

Nevada 4

Utah 5

Arizona 8

Montana 3

Wyoming 3

Colorado 8

Alaska 3

Missouri 11

North Dakota 3

South Dakota 3

Nebraska 5

Kansas 6

Oklahoma 8

Texas 32

Arkansas 6

Louisiana 9

Indiana 12

Ohio 21

West Virginia 5

Virginia 13

North Carolina 14

Tennessee 11

Mississippi 7

Alabama 9

Georgia 13

South Carolina 8

Florida 25

Kentucky 8

New Hampshire 4

Total 271 votes

Gore

Hawaii 4

Washington 11

Oregon 7

California 54

New Mexico 5

Minnesota 10

Iowa 7

Wisconsin 11

Illinois 22

Michigan 18

Maine 4

Vermont 3

New York 33

Pennsylvania 23

District of Columbia 3

Maryland 10

Delaware 3

New Jersey 15

Connecticut 8

Rhode Island 4

Massachusetts 12

Total 267 votes